Our Voices

Our Voices

SIX WOMEN WITH MULTIPLE PERSONALITIES TALK ABOUT LIFE AND RELATIONSHIPS IN THEIR MIDLIFE

• • •

Elizabeth M. W.-B. Green, PhD

LCMHC, MA, NCC, DCC, MFLC

ISBN-13: 9781533000071
ISBN-10: 1533000077
Library of Congress Control Number: 2016907387
CreateSpace Independent Publishing Platform
North Charleston, South Carolina

Contents

Acknowledgments

● ● ●

I wish to thank my husband, BNG, for encouraging me before, during, and through the process of this endeavor. Without his unflagging optimism, humor, and belief in me, this project would not have survived.

The six women, Jaybee, Sarah I, Sarah II, Eve, Mato, and Betty deserve a standing ovation for their willingness to participate and their joyful optimism that, when heard, their collective heard voices will make a difference in the professional and public communities. I also thank my clients, past and present, with DID, who have taught me and continue to teach me the art of listening and connecting on many levels. I am honored that I have been entrusted with this mission.

My transcriptionist, WBC, put in uncountable hours transcribing the taped interviews. I also thank CF, who worked with me in organizing the volume of research data.

Introduction

• • •

A PROJECT WAS CONDUCTED WITH six midlife women with Dissociative Identity Disorder (DID, formerly known as MPD [Multiple Personality Disorder]). The women shared four criteria: gender, DID, midlife, and fiscal independence. The purpose was to focus on whether or not midlife had a major impact on internal and/or external relationships, and if so, how.

The findings did not support the assumption that, for women with DID, midlife would be a major factor in dealing with the consequences of this lifelong defense mechanism. Midlife was viewed as part of the process of life and not as a pivotal point in their lives.

Analysis of the collective data suggested that validation, respect, acceptance, and nonjudgmental regard within relationships were the primary issues that impacted their internal and external relationships across their lifespan, not just in midlife.

The six women unanimously expressed a strong desire for their voices and perspectives to be heard by the public and the mental health professions. That desire is the reason for this book—to let others know their own views and experiences.

The states of grace these six women have attained in spite of the overwhelming events of their lives is humbling. These survivors of the cruelty of childhood traumas; years of misdiagnosis; and misunderstanding by professionals, family, and the public are a testament to the resiliency of the human spirit. To simplify, minimize, or glamorize DID would be an insult and disservice to the women and men with DID and to the clinicians who work with them and believe in the capacity of the human spirit to survive and thrive.

The interviews are respectful of the seriousness of the diagnosis, its cause, and the enormity of the healing process. These women only wanted a respectful and credible forum within which to have the reality of their lives heard in their own words, to offer encouragement to others with DID, to demystify DID for the public and to help the professional community to be more open to their personal experience in assessing and working with the person who comes to them with DID.

CHAPTER 1

Introduction

● ● ●

TODAY, THERE IS A WIDE range of information available about the midlife stage of development for women. It is difficult to pinpoint an exact age when "midlife" begins, but different sources generally agree that the middle years begin in the forties. Gail Sheehy (1995) states, "No one can really be certain anymore when he or she hits the midpoint" (p. 57). Gloria Steinem (1992) talks about the aging process, midlife, and how she became aware of her own process at about fifty, when she noticed bodily changes such as facial lines, thinning hair, "age spots" on her hands, and so forth. Joan Borysenko (1996) suggests that women go through "the midlife metamorphosis," a midlife transitional stage, between the ages of forty-two and forty-nine. Daniel J. Levinson (1996) states that the "era of middle adulthood" for men and women is between the ages of forty and sixty-five.

These researchers agree that midlife is a time when women and men seem to evaluate the physical, financial, emotional, and spiritual quality of their lives, choosing or not to choose to make conscious changes in lifestyle as they move into their later adult years. These years seem to be a time of psychological reflection, even as life is complicated with the tasks of career adjustments, grown children, aging parents, and personal health issues.

My feeling is that midlife is personally defined by each woman and man. For women, it may begin with the onset of the pre-menopausal phase of life, which varies with each woman, depending on her genetic map. It is generally accepted that the premenopausal phase begins in the early forties (sometimes earlier) and lasts ten or more years with menopause (cessation of the menstrual cycle) being somewhere in one's fifties. I am not sure using the biological markers of perimenopause and menopause to identify midlife for women is an appropriate measure. Perhaps midlife is more a feeling or recognition of change than a measurable entity. For men and women, midlife may not be easy to pinpoint with a biological marker but defined more in terms of longevity; life expectancy; and quality of life, in terms of physical, spiritual, emotional, and financial factors.

How the Topic Emerged

When I first came to the field of counseling psychology, I was not prepared for the personal, intellectual, and emotional challenges involved with working with survivors of long term childhood sexual and physical assault. My first internship was a trial by fire as I was handed caseloads of women of all ages diagnosed with Borderline Personality Disorder, Major Depression, Eating Disorders, Obsessive-Compulsive Personality Disorder, and often a combination of these diagnoses. These were exciting women and men to be with in the therapy hours and at times terrifying, because it was so clear to me how little I knew.

During the period of my graduate internship, my clientele taught me the art of listening with my eyes, ears, mind, heart, and intuition. Several times, I thought their symptoms added up to their diagnoses and more, but as an intern, I was told it would be professional suicide to disagree with the psychiatrists. In group case presentations, I tentatively suggested that perhaps Client A had Multiple Personality Disorder (now known as Dissociative Identity Disorder) in addition to the other diagnoses. It was a professional risk that I have never regretted taking.

Even after my internship I continued to work with a few men and many women survivors of chronic childhood trauma, and I have found that some survivors have degrees of a dissociative disorder from mild to severe. There was no definitive line of either/or, but more of a continuum between mild and severe. I also observed that some of my clients with dissociative disorders had varying degrees of functionality. The phrase "varying degrees of functionality" falls on a continuum paralleling the mild/severe continuum of the diagnosis.

I recognized the basic diagnostic patterns of DID but noted the complex uniqueness of each person. I heard many times from these women who had been able to function well enough to stay fiscally independent of the social service network that "nobody gets it," especially those professionals in the mental health community.

It is important to understand that DID is not a description of several different personalities, as the historical fiction and nonfiction presented in the early years. As time passed it became clear that the person seeming to have different personalities actually had one personality that was fractured into however many parts were needed to survive the horrors the person was repeatedly enduring. Think of holding a mirror and dropping it. It shatters into multiple pieces, but it is still one mirror, albeit broken.

The application of the scientific method to the dissociative disorders has encouraged the evolution of treatment modalities: ideally, with measurable objectives for the person so diagnosed. The research literature on DID has been written by non-dissociative people informing the professional community about people with DID whose symptoms could be statistically separated, measured, and categorized. Instruments of measurement have been created that place people with DID into neat categories, boxes. This is not a criticism, as this process was necessary and has helped provide general descriptions, language, treatment guidelines, and treatment outcomes.

However, the use of a statistical, quantitative model of research tends to reduce and judge the complexities of life experiences, and "so long as the statistics of normalizing developmental psychology determine the standards against which the extraordinary complexities of a life are judged, deviations become deviants" (Hillman, 1996, p. 30, p.30). The phenomenological approach does not place a barrier between the primary researcher and the co-researcher enabling the flavor of the experience of being a midlife woman with Dissociative Identity Disorder to be uncensored.

Goals

This project is a phenomenological research study focusing on midlife women with DID who have been able to function relatively well in the context of their professional, social, and familial relationships. When they enter their middle years (thirty-five to sixty-five years of age), things seem to change in terms of adequate functioning in interpersonal and inter-institutional relationships. Throughout their lives, these women have had relational problems, but my clinical observation has been that there is a difference in the quality of the midlife relationships. The relational dilemmas occur internally within their systems of personality parts and externally within their social networks.

I discerned these qualitative differences from their own statements, as told to me during the course of our clinical relationships. During my clinical experience working with midlife women with Dissociative Identity Disorder, a universal statement kept being expressed. The women seemed to feel as if "I'm going crazy," "I'm losing control," "I'm losing it," and "It wasn't like this before." What was different for them—why now? Was there a common denominator for these women that made the difference within their current internal and external relationships?

The women to whom I refer did share several common denominators: middle age, histories of severe childhood abuse, psychotherapy, and relational difficulties with people and institutions. These women were not incapacitated to the point of dependency on the network of state and/or federal social services agencies. They had been able to maintain financial independence through employment and to have interpersonal relationships, which were often chaotic and inappropriate, but manageable. Their DID was not as florid as the well-known cases of Sybil (Schreiber, 1973), Eve (Sizemore, 1989; Thigpen & Cleckley, 1957), Billy (Keyes, 1981), or Trudie (Chase, 1987).

These midlife women with whom I worked felt they had been able to maintain tolerable lifestyles with periods of disruption and chaos. They had enjoyed a measure of success in spite of the DID and its associated problems in all areas of life. Now in their middle years, things were different, and this time they felt as if they would not be able to maintain the same level of control as they had in the past. They all felt that if something did not change, they would lose control of their internal and external worlds—they really would "go crazy." *It*, defined as the internal and external life, was not the same for them.

This led me to wonder if there is a common factor of midlife that in some way had an impact on their internal relationships with their personality parts and their external relationships with other people.

So the question that has led me to this phenomenological research project is born from my long term work with midlife women with DID is this: Do the midlife stages of development influence or change external and internal relationships for women with DID? To find the answer, it was necessary to ask women in midlife with DID if midlife does have an effect on their internal and/or external relationships. They are the sources, and they are the experts on this phenomenon.

SOCIAL RELEVANCY

Although there has been an increase in the professional literature on DID in the past fifteen to twenty plus years, I have not found anything that specifically addresses this perspective. The question about the influence of midlife on internal and external relationships for this population is socially relevant for the following reasons:

First, this project is grounded in inductive reasoning (a logical process in which select premises are assumed to be true or at least often true), and the findings may further explicate information unique to midlife women in general and the effect of midlife on their personal relationships. Second, this project will provide in-depth information from a phenomenological perspective on and for women with DID.

A phenomenological approach to a question about a diagnosis as complex as DID keeps the focus on the importance of the person as a human being and does not reduce the person to an objectified, measurable quantity in order to support a specific developmental paradigm. Hillman (1996) commented that "So long as the statistics of normalizing developmental psychology determine the standards against which the extraordinary complexities of a life are judged, and deviations become deviants" (p. 30).

Another potential by-product of this project may be to help those in the professional community keep the focus on the client as having a diagnosis and not *being* a diagnosis, which challenges the treating·professional to make a commitment to a long-term therapeutic relationship. Treating professionals may need to reevaluate their standards of care and choose between honoring a commitment to their client as a unique human being or a commitment to a third-party payer paradigm of treatment that focuses on measurable outcomes within severe time constraints. In those situations the treatment is compromised and meets the needs of the third party.

THE QUESTION

How does midlife impact the external and internal relationships for a woman with Dissociative Identity Disorder when she is in her midlife journey?

Much of the literature concerned with midlife for women in general focuses on menopause and the premenopausal years, indicating that this has a negative impact on quality of life and relationships. Until the women's movement of the 1970s and 1980s, this had been considered a time when women in general developed physical and emotional problems due to an aging, changing body, with decreasing sexuality and physical attractiveness, plus a feeling of uselessness as the children left home.

The assumptions about this period in a woman's life were predominately posited by men with a psychodynamic theoretical orientation (Greer, 1992; Steinem, 1992) and did not portray women in a positive manner. Today, the general view has changed. With women's increased life expectancy now eighty years or older, the premenopausal years are more of a transitional phase of transition into mature middle age than a discrete stage of life for women (Levinson, 1996; Sheehy, 1995). Midlife is more than a biological change for women but is, as Greer (1992) states, "a time of stocktaking, of spiritual as well as physical change, and it would be a pity to be unconscious of it" (pg. 5).

The woman with DID experiences herself as having different personalities, which may be the result of popular myths or legends. The accepted research data states that there is only one personality per person (Ross 1997), but that the one personality can alter or be divided, split, sectioned, or compartmentalized into many segments, parts, or components), or alters. It is important to note that the professional community has developed the language for describing the dissociative process, but the descriptors the person with DID uses may be different from and even contradictory to the professional terms.

My clinical experience in working with dissociation indicates that each internal system has its own organization, and the components may or may not have a relationship with some or all of the other internal parts. The general pattern of organization for a DID system is basically similar for most people, but there is a unique twist to presentations of DID, which contributes to the difficulty of making an early accurate diagnosis.

The external relationships a woman with DID has are often contingent upon her internal relationships. They are connected, but exactly how is still an area that needs exploration. I suspect that they run parallel courses (i.e., when external relationships are relatively functional, then internal relationships are also relatively functional, and vice versa). Therefore, it is logical not to separate the impact the mercurial midlife process may have on internal and external relationships.

It is important to understand that relationships within and without may not be healthy collectively and/or individually. Again, I reiterate that this unique defense system was developed for the survival of the whole personality. The relationship models upon which various parts of the system have been designed may or may not have been functional. Each part has a defined job within the system, and there may be a variety of genders and races and a range of ages. Sometimes the internal system is vast with many pieces, even blocks of robotic mechanisms designed to protect the core personality and maintain safety.

The purpose of this book is about the women with DID who have and are living the experience of midlife, and if midlife effects their internal and/or external relationships as the questions suggest. By approaching the collected data with a minimal amount of preconceived judgment, I hope their own words will report their perspectives on this particular topic.

DEFINITION OF SOME TERMS

DID (DISSOCIATIVE IDENTITY DISORDER)

DID as defined by the mental health professional community is the fragmentation (splitting) of an individual's personality into two or more distinct components (parts), which alternate behavioral control, depending on the immediate situation.

How

In the question on the previous page—"How does midlife impact the external and internal relationships for women with DID?"—the word *how* is used because my assumption suggests that midlife does, indeed, have a significant impact on relationships for all women, whether or not they have a diagnosis of DID. Literature on midlife suggests that women do experience changes in relationships. Personally, I believe that midlife is a relative term, subject to individual qualities and parameters, but for the sake of clarity, I define midlife as the period of time between the ages of thirty-five and sixty-five.

Internal Relationships

These are the relationships among the personality components, aka alters.

External Relationships

This term refers to the woman's alters' (personality components') external interactions with people and the environment. People without divided, fractured personalities have external relationships and interactions experienced as a whole.

CHAPTER 2

A Brief History of Dissociative Disorders

● ● ●

THE PHENOMENON OF DISSOCIATIVE DISORDERS has been documented throughout history. In Europe during the 1880s, Pierre Janet made the connection between severe childhood trauma and dissociation. He is credited with first using the term "dissociation" as it is used today (Crabtree, 1992; van der Hart, 1996). The European and US professional communities generally agreed that dissociation was a defense mechanism in response to childhood trauma. Respected people like William James, Sigmund Freud, and Morton Prince wrote and published accounts of multiple personality disorders (now known as DID) (Crabtree, 1985, 1993; Kluft & Fine, 1993), supporting Janet's connection of this disorder to severe, chronic childhood trauma (Crabtree,1992; Rivera,1996; van der Kolk & van der Hart, 1991).

Under pressure from his peers, Freud abandoned the unpopular trauma based theory of dissociation and focused attention on his Oedipal Complex, psychosexual theory of development and his seduction theory. This direction was more "politically correct" for the times and was embraced by the psychoanalytically trained psychiatrists of the early twentieth century. Janet's theory slid into obscurity, resulting in the diagnosis of many trauma survivors with an organic brain syndrome instead of Dissociative Identity Disorder (at that time known as Multiple Personality Disorder) (Ross, 1997). Even today it is estimated that 25 percent to 49 percent of clients with DID are initially diagnosed with schizophrenia (Gainer, 1994).

Despite the documentation of severe dissociative disorders in the history of psychiatry and psychology for more than one hundred years, it has only been in the past twenty five or so years that the mental health community has begun to come to a consensus about the etiology of DID. There continues to be debate about the authenticity of DID. Ross (1997) makes the point that DID is not literally real. It is not possible to have more than one person in the same body. People with DID do not have more than one personality. Not believing in DID is like not believing in hallucinations. All psychiatrists believe in hallucinations and elusions, grasp the fact that hallucinations and delusions are not real, and understand that they are real psychiatric symptoms (p.64).

DID is a complex defense mechanism caused by inescapable trauma (Briere, 1997; Chu & Dill, 1990; Kluft, 1984a, 1984b; Putnam, 1989a; 1989b; Ross, 1989, 1997; Wilbur, 1985) with no resource for external healing or nurturing relationships (Chu & Dill, 1990; Crabtree, 1992; Kluft & Fine, 1993; Putnam, 1989a; Ross, 1994,1997). The more severe and chronic the trauma, the more complex the dissociative disorder (Ross, 1994; Ross et al; van der Kolk, 1987).

Aside from the debate over authenticity of the condition, DID is difficult to diagnose accurately due to the diversity of symptom presentation and overlap with other clinical diagnoses, such as Borderline Personality Disorder, Obsessive-Compulsive Personality Disorder, Bipolar and Major Depressions, Schizophrenia, chemical abuse, and other addictive problems (Kluft,, 1984a,1991; O'Brien, 1985). Putnam (1989a) notes that the accurate diagnosis of DID usually does not occur until the person is in his/her thirties or forties.

Some researchers have documented that DID is more common than formerly believed (Putnam, 1989a;Putnam, Guroff, Silberman, Barban, & Post, 1986; Ross, Anderson, Fleisher, & Norton, 1991; Ross, Norton, & Fraser, 1989; Schultz, Braun, & Kluft, 1989). Ross et al. (1992) suggest that 1 percent of the population may have DID and that dissociative disorders in general may affect up to 10 percent of the population of the United States. Based on general characteristics, the professional community has been able to establish guidelines by which the clinician can identify categories of dissociation. This type of personality disturbance is not related to the effects of organic disease, head trauma, or excessive chemical usage.

Some of the personality parts have differences in physiological functions (e.g. one part may have diabetic symptoms, and another may not). There may be a difference in vision and hearing among personality parts. There may be a high tolerance to physical pain; a history of severe headaches; problems with asthma; and/or reproductive and bowel problems that do not affect all of the personality parts.

SOME THEORIES OF DEVELOPMENT

Most of the traditional theories of general development are based on studies of men (Miller & Stiver, 1997). Women have not been included in many research studies, even though the results of these studies have been generalized to women. Belenky, Clinchy, Goldberger, and Tarule (1986) comment succinctly that "developmental theory has established men's experience and competence as a baseline against which both men's and women's development is then judged, often to the detriment or misreading of women" (p.7).

The process of change in psychological developmental theories began with the eventual breaking away from Freud's psychosexual theory of development to a more relational view, still based on biological needs. Each reworking of the material and manipulation of data and ideas of psychological development added another level of knowledge based on data gathered from the study of the male gender and generalized to the female gender.

Contemporary writers, such as Levinson and Sheehy, refined and expanded previous theories to cover today's longer life span. People's life span has increased from forty-seven years to eighty-four (in those who survive to sixty-five). Sheehy and Levinson have each added to the popular vocabulary and language of developmental theory and have given us terms such as "passage to the age of mastery" and "the Samson complex" (Sheehy, 1995) and "transitional phases" and "life structures" (Levinson, 1996). Sheehy acknowledges gender differences and the impact of the women's movement on the paradigm shifts in psychology. She expanded her stages of adult life through the eighties and beyond, designating ages eighteen to thirty as "provisional adulthood and forty-five to eighty-five and older as "first adulthood." Each stage has developmental goals and crises associated with it (Sheehy, 1995).

Levinson supports the concept of developmental tasks and renegotiating relationships throughout the life process. Though he does not cite the Stone Center relational model in his work, he does incorporate some of its concepts of mutuality and relationship. He reworked and reorganized Erikson's adult developmental stages into nine stages, including transitional phases.

Bowlby's work was important in bringing attention to the relationship aspect of development throughout life. It is not a staged development but pathways that are determined by the relationship a person has with his or her environment in the moment (Bowlby,1988). Environment is dynamic and defined as the interactions and behaviors among people within a relationship. The potential to change into whatever form is necessary in reaction to an adverse environment is a strong drive to survive.

The Stone Center at Wellesley College supported scholars Judith Jordan, Alexandra G. Kaplan, Jean Baker Miller, Irene P. Stiver, and Janet L. Surrey, who shared insights and thoughts on their conception of women's development. The Stone Center scholars, over a long period of time, have questioned the traditional psychoanalytic theories, which "reflect societal and cultural assumptions so deeply entrenched in all of us that we scarcely question their validity, we simply think of them as 'the truth' about human development" (Miller & Stiver, 1997, p. 2). Through their respective professional and clinical work, they have come to formulate a developmental paradigm for women, which challenges the traditional psychodynamic school of thought.

The relational model of the Stone Center explores the importance of connection in relationships for women throughout their lives. This particular model of relationship addresses separation, individuation, connection, and reconnection as happening within mutually empathic and enhancing relationships, across the life cycle. Miller (1976) states that "women's sense of self becomes very much organized around being able to make and then to maintain affiliation and relationships" (p. 83). The appropriate, healthy interaction with others helps us to create relational images that are "patterns of relational experiences" (Miller & Stiver, 1997, p. 40) that are internalized and against which we measure and judge future interactions. Internal mental health problems can occur with an external manifestation or manifestations, which may take a variety of expressions if there are repeated disconnections throughout life.

A sense of self revolves around being able to make and maintain strong, appropriate relationships with others, beginning in infancy (Miller, 1976, p. 83). Psychological problems are a result of repeated and multiple disconnections and insults to the core being within a toxic relationship and interactions. This may lead to poor connections with relationships beginning in early childhood. As this type of toxic relationship with others continues to evolve, it becomes a one-sided relationship wherein one person tries to fulfill the expectations of the other in order to obtain some form of attachment. Particular patterns of attachment are formed and replicated throughout the life span. This is true for the strong, healthy, mutually enhancing connection and the opposite pattern of attachment.

This chapter is an abbreviated and simplified presentation of a few developmental paradigms. If you are interested in the more complex areas of developmental theories, there is much more available in the literature.

The Interview Data

● ● ●

THE SIX WOMEN WHO PARTICIPATED in this project had common themes. Most of the women quickly expanded beyond the original research question and incorporated and shared their essential experiences of having DID. Each had expressed enthusiastic willingness to participate in this project, coupled with a deep desire to help explain to the professional community and the public what dissociation is like for the woman who manages her life relatively well.

The age range was between thirty-eight and sixty-two years, representing the full spectrum of the midlife years as discussed in Chapter 3. Each woman chose her pseudonym, and any specifically identifying information is a composite. The educational levels ranged from high school graduate with continuing education to graduate degrees. All of these women had worked in a professional environment at some point in their lives. Two women have chosen to no longer work in that environment but to pursue other areas that express their creative interests. One of the women, Sarah 1, has maintained consistent employment for more than ten years and was promoted within her company, even though she had several hospitalizations related to her therapeutic process.

Five out of the six women were diagnosed with DID in their thirties. The clinicians who made the diagnoses all admitted to not having worked knowingly with a client with DID in the past, but they were willing to learn. All five of these women are currently with the therapists who made their DID diagnoses. The sixth woman, Jaybee, who is sixty-two years old, was not correctly diagnosed until three years ago. Only Jaybee had a significant therapeutic history before being correctly diagnosed, which included Paranoid Schizophrenia, Major Depression, and Bipolar and Borderline Personality Disorders, and she was placed on a number of psychotropic medications. Today, Jaybee is medication free and functioning well.

Four of the women are married, with no previous marriages. Two have young children living at home; one has stepchildren not living with her and spouse; and one woman has grown children living outside of the home. One woman was married in her twenties and divorced with no children, and one woman has had a long-term partner. The four married women indicate that their marital relationships are stable, but they have all experienced challenging periods over the course of the relationships.

The text that is italicized contains verbatim excerpts. To maintain the flow and flavor of the stories, the "ums," "ahs," "uhs," and repetitive words are not included. Clarifications are in brackets; each story begins with a brief composite biographical sketch.

The chapter will conclude with an interpretive synthesis of the six major themes. The eloquence of these amazing women is evident in their communication styles.

JAYBEE

Jaybee, at sixty-two years of age, is the eldest of the six women in this project. She is a childless, single woman who has had several long-term relationships but is not currently in a romantic relationship. Jaybee has worked in the corporate world, although she now chooses to work as a groundskeeper, carpenter, and artist. She talks about the process of change across her lifespan, beginning in her early thirties.

She has a long history with the mental health community and was incorrectly diagnosed with schizophrenia, borderline personality disorder, bipolar disorder, depression and other mental health problems. She was given psychotropic medications over the years. She was not diagnosed with DID until three years ago, when she began therapy with her present therapist, who had never worked with someone with DID.

The interview began with the query about whether midlife had an impact on internal and external relationships and, if so, how? The probe questions were interspersed to help maintain focus.

I see my early thirties, I was a lot angrier...there was a lot of activity going on inside. Because there was a lot of stress, I worked the corporate world and being a woman, things weren't quite fair. Everybody just did dumb things, you know? [This is in reference to her internal system.]

Just a lot of outbursts...a lot of anger...a lot of turmoil with external relationships. I thought I was crazy to tell the truth, because everybody told me I was, so I had to believe what the adults would say. But I think, I mean, it was something different, but like I said, I always thought it was me. I thought I made these people up, and I made them come through, and I thought it was me, because I, because they said it was me, so, it wasn't until I was in probably my thirties when I, in the sixties, started to read "Seth." I do feel different, I mean, as far as my midlife, you know, stages: I still made enemies, I still made friends, still made assholes of all of us. [Her internal personality parts.]

Jaybee found through her reading of the "Seth" books by Jane Roberts during her thirties and forties a certain acceptance and understanding of herself. The premise of the books is that Jane Roberts (the author) is a channel for an entity named Seth. Seth speaks about being on different levels of reality, afterlife, karma, life choices, and spiritual guides.

I related there and would be able…to say that it wasn't me, that we were a multi-dimensional person, and I was able to accept it, but I still wasn't able to relate it. Because there was no one out there to relate it to…and if there was, they certainly weren't talking about it…and people thought I was eccentric, weird, all of those titles. I really didn't understand much of what was going on, and I really thought there was something radically wrong with me. It really didn't change, like I said, until about the late sixties, when I first picked up Jane Roberts, and I could relate, and I was like wow, whew! This is not me, this is JUST not me.

I asked Jaybee if she had ever read any material specifically about DID and if so, if the information had changed her self-perception.

Not really…just Jane Roberts. I mean, I've tried, but nothing really gels with me. Nothing gives me the feeling that Jane Roberts…how she communicates, and I'm able to relate to them. I have tried, and nothing seems to make it. It seems like primary reading after reading Seth…Everything seems like reading a kindergarten book or something. Doesn't have the depth—boring! That's another thing I have a problem with—that other stuff is written by, they don't get it. [Jaybee was making reference to professional and popular literature that she has tried to read in the past. She suggested that being able to relate to Jane Roberts's experiences of being a channel for the entity Seth and her age contributed to self-acceptance.]

It's probably a combination, but I would say it would be a combination of experience and just living it, and trying to understand: trying to get some sense out of it.

As stated previously, her experiences with the mental health profession had been a series of misdiagnoses and excessive medication. Her current therapist was new to DID.

So, I never, ever talked about it to anybody until Sue [pseudonym for her current therapist]. *We're* [alters] *all feeling safer with who we are, each and every one of us. Because we've been accepted…We've accepted ourselves and Sue has accepted us. I have some other friends that have accepted me and all of us* [alters].*…So I think that acceptance alone has calmed us down. Acceptance is very important, I think, for all of us* [alters]. *Validity, you know. That's the whole thing. Being validated, when there's a negative connotation on you for sixty years, all of us, not* *just me. We're all in that bracket, and so we're all beat down for those many years, and then finally, you get WHOA! You know, we are A-OK, we ARE. We are accepted, and we are. We're not murderers, we're not rapists, WE'RE NOT!*

There was no acceptance on the outside, so that certainly did make a mark on the inside. Since being with Sue, the validity gave us a feeling of worth; there was something there and we feel more comfortable, and we feel like we're OK. It's OK, and there's lots of us [alters], and no problem. We don't have to be off-the-wall.

The following monologue indicates self-responsibility, along with acceptance and validation:

I'll go back with this Seth thing, that it's helped all of us, too, because on another level, we all know that we are what we think, each one of us, all of us. We are what we think. And what I think, the main person—that's me—certainly does affect all of us. So my goal with Sue is to change my thought patterns, which is extremely hard. I'm the motor, the engine, the one that cuts through the physical plane. I'm the one that has to deal with everybody and everything—sort of like a mediator, because I'm able to sit and talk to them, really get down and dirty with them. I'm more mature in life experiences, of growing. I guess becoming a little more at ease with that process of totally accepting life as what you make it.

In her forties, Jaybee found herself changing internally, which affected her external relationships. She concludes with a statement of self-responsibility:

The emotions are still there...The aggressions are still there, the anger is still there, the outbursts are still there. My going away is still there, and maybe in my forties, it lessened. I mean, becoming a lot less, and we were beginning to attract different types of people. A lot of reading of Roberts in our forties, and I was seeing a little bit of change within all of us, because we were relating. As we change, the physical individual started changing, and everybody else kind of follows, because it's a sort of domino effect, the core belief system is changing, and so they all start to change, and in those changes, the energies are changing. So we're not attracting the people that are angry anymore, and so as our lives are growing older, we're starting to attract more people in the arts and teaching, instead of the no-brainers sitting around smoking and drinking. We started to change, all of us. We started to bring in a different group of people from the outside.

In the following passage, Jaybee uses the metaphor of sculpting to explain her evolution and acceptance of personal responsibility for the formulation of her life as she ages:

I'm thoroughly enjoying it now, in these years. Yeah, definitely, thoroughly enjoying it. It's like being in school, being in an art class, you know, sculpting my whole new life. That's what it feels like. It's kind of fun, because I've always sculpted such ugly things in the past, not always, but in a lot of relationships. But now my sculpting of life is becoming a little more refined...Sometimes I think it will show up in my art. I'm the master, I'm responsible for the outcome. It's a work in progress. It's like you still have the same tools, you still have the same colors, just in the way you're mixing them and using them...all those tools...You know, it's like a piece of wood...You get this chunk of wood, and it's all squared, and I finished putting some curves and lines in it and planes of life, kind of, you know, a period of your life, you're probably very angular, extremely angular and sharp and abrupt, and things just sort of [She makes a slashing sound] *and as you grow older, things start to become rounded and molded and deeper and you don't have surface cuts and surface planes that are taken off, but going deeper inside, molding, rounding the out taking off all the rough edges and...*[She sighs.]

Jaybee talks about appreciating herself, her internal parts, and their differences. She has no desire to integrate—merge the parts—but wants the
alters to continue grow.

We all experience the same things [referring to external people], *and it's
part of life, only I just sometimes experience them with a different being*
[alter]. *The perception, I guess that's what it would be. They'll* [the alters]
*never leave; I don't want them to ever leave, but I want them to learn and
continue to learn. Appreciation just sort of happened. We're becoming more
and more in love with each other—it's frightening.* [She laughs.]

I asked Jaybee if, as her body ages, anything changes for her, internally or
externally.

*Naw, does it stop you from doing things? You know, here you are, you're
sixty-two and this sixteen-year-old wants to come out right now and do
things that a sixty-two-year-old body shouldn't be doing. But I can do
them. Smoke a joint, any of that stuff. No, they don't change. They're still
kids—I don't know; I grow old, but they still get to stay—you know—
that's kind of mean, because they get to stay those little things, teenagers,
or adults. But they get to stay there for some reason. Why that happens, I
don't understand. That I don't understand. Why don't they get to grow*

with me? They always stay there, just stay there, Hmmm, maybe that's where they stopped in time.

There are times I have a different feeling bodywise. Physical feelings—sometimes I feel larger, like wrists that are larger and my hands will feel much bigger, or widthwise, or I feel a little taller, or I feel small, or different kinds of feelings that go with different entities.

From here, Jaybee began to talk about her spirituality aspect and her appreciation of being able to identify parallel perceptions.

We're doing a lot more [sigh], can't say spiritual, can't say mental, because it's beyond that, it's deeper than spiritual, or deeper than mental, but it seems like a plane or something—on a different plane. There are times when I might be looking at something—all of a sudden, the thing no longer was what I was looking at, because whoever was looking at it with me changed the whole picture of the design. It's delightful! It's the perception.

When I asked Jaybee if she thought she was any different today than she was forty years ago, she offered the following insights:

I think so. It's like I said before, because the energies that are generated by all of us are much more peaceful and much more reasonable, much more understanding of others. But yeah, I think in my case, anyway, it's getting better; it's getting better for the people on the outside of me and getting better for the people inside of me.

This concludes Jaybee's interview.

MATO

Mato is a married mental-health professional with grown children. She is approximately fifty years old and admittedly is in menopause. She does not have a long history of psychotherapy and currently sees her therapist on an as-needed basis. She has had no hospitalizations for mental health issues.

We started the interview with a review of the parameters to maintain confidentiality and the purpose of the project. She had read the guide questions and had made notes on what she wanted to say. She needed little prompting or refocusing.

Midlife? Yes, it has [changed me] *in a number of ways. Physically, with menopause, I gained sixty pounds had to deal with the hot flashes—I find that very difficult, very triggering for different parts of me. I don't like to be hot, I don't like to sweat. That's a trigger for me often, so that kind of thing, especially if I'm at work and trying to function at some meeting or group, or if I'm in a team meeting, so it's really hard. It takes a lot of energy to refocus. The weight gain has been horrendous...five pounds a week for sixty pounds. It seemed to be triggered by menopause, but I was also on medication, and I think they went hand in hand, and I've always been thin my entire life, I was underweight. Also, in the midlife time I kind of got the empty nest syndrome that everybody goes through...I have five surviving children, having them go through their issues, leave the house, having guilt because even though I did the best I could, I have to wonder how I affected each one of them, my kids, in good and bad ways. My youngest is getting her doctorate at a very young age. My middle child works in mental health and is back home temporarily, because it's convenient.*

The empty nest stuff, even though I've got the two [large animals], keeping me pretty busy, I still miss the children. I love my children, and as much as I think I might want them home, I wouldn't want them home [laughs], but it's a struggle that I think everybody goes through...The body changes, the memory...forget the memory...The memory is very difficult for me, because I don't know if it's from all the head traumas that have finally caught up with me, because I had a broken neck, or if it's menopause, or if I'm dissociating. It's hard to tell; sometimes it's just very hard to tell, which is frustrating more than anything else. Stress would have bothered me prior to midlife...maybe it doesn't affect me the same way, and I feel a little bit more empowered at this point. I did work through so many of my issues, and because I was able and because I was able to let stuff go, and because there are times in life I can feel really positive about what I'm able to do, and also to see my kids have human problems but also work them through and know it's part of life.

And I go around in circles with a lot of this, and that's part of my selves, talking through...I'll blame myself, and then I'll say, "But look at how good they're doing, and they'd be neurotic if everything was perfect" and just go round and round, till I'm exhausted and then try to do something else. [She laughs.]

Oh, the menopause. I think I must have been pushed into an earlier menopause...I think the trauma, the physical and emotional trauma gave me an earlier menopause. So it's still the friggin' hot flashes. The weight gain and hot flashes...I can't believe it! [She laughs.] *It's very hard to maintain the health professional part of me when I get triggered in a meeting because of the hot flashes. Have somebody younger be triggered! You know what I mean? And still maintain who I am and what I'm there for...It's very difficult. But now I can do it—I'm more mature. So much has changed in my profession that's, that's nasty. And waking up at forty, fifty years old, and all of a sudden being that adult, feeling like I never had a childhood, has been hard.*

At this point, Mato talks about how she copes with not having had a childhood.

But I found a way around it...getting the two [large animals] and a couple of times not accepting that I'm always fifty, I'm gonna be fifty, but I'm gonna go out and raise hell with my sister. I play; I play a lot. I play with my two [large animals] a lot. At midlife when some people are toning down a little bit, I'm getting more active. Because we hike twelve miles three times a week with them. I usually spend my summers outside. I feel healthier than I did, even though I've gained this nasty weight.

Mato spoke often about her spiritual side being the piece that has helped her maintain balance and support throughout her life.

To have a little more time to nurture myself, to go swimming or whatever, to really refocus on my spiritual side. Sometimes, this kind of goes along with what I just said, a lot of survival skills that just happened may continue to happen on an everyday basis...and that is exhausting. I guess the struggle is to keep that balance, because of being middle aged. I can work and be focused and function and feel good about that and then have a day off. So it's hard to keep that balance and remind myself. But don't we all struggle with something emotional or whatever? It's just my inner self, plus going through the therapy was like I was on a very high spiritual level.

Mato continued to explain her spiritual side and how her therapist infringed on her boundaries, which dampened her spirituality for a period of time, until she withdrew from therapy.

I had a bear tooth that was gifted to me, and he [the therapist] had admired it and always wanted my bear tooth…So we'd kind of switch every visit. He'd take the bear tooth to wear, and it'd be like that spiritual connection, which felt like a boundary issue to the spiritual Native American part of me. The bear tooth had been gifted to me, because my power animal is the bear. That always gave me strength and a reminder of something I could grasp onto, and at first it was OK for him to take it, but then I felt very violated like that was mine, and I didn't like his energy. His thought was, well, he was safe, that's what he verbalized. My feeling was like "No, thank you." When I left, I took it back, it still doesn't feel like it's mine anymore. And you know I cleansed it, but it feels like even the bear was drained from it. It was like somebody who didn't know what they were using it for, which is OK. Life happens.

She continued to discuss her spiritual side and how it has been a source of strength and guidance for her, especially now.

I think that one of my elders that I journey to [a Native American ritual] was the one who was always there when I was younger. When I would journey every once in a while, I would see her, and she would look very angry, like, "What are you doing? When are you going...We've got things to do." And at one point, she even had her back turned to me, like, "I've had enough. Are you gonna stay with this crap forever, or are you gonna move on?"

One time, I was journeying, and I ended up in a tepee with her, and she was offering me something. My sense was she was showing me some kind of healing. I was supposed to shut up and listen to what she had to say. At one point, I asked her who she was, because the name that I use now when I do some medicine work is X and I said, "Who are you?" Because I've seen her so many times, and she just said, "I am you," so, I don't know—inner self, another lifetime—it doesn't really matter. She's part of me, it's a strength thing. I have a lot of peace; I think that and the fact that, again, I've worked with so many issues and have made peace with a lot of my abusers and have made peace in my own head.

Mato spoke at length about how her American Indian parts have been with her since she was a child, and how these parts have always served her well. She has chosen to continue to live her life in cooperation with her parts.

I know some people who have multiple personalities or dissociative disorder or different parts or whatever you want to call it, have this fear that as they heal or get better or integrate, they feel like they're killing their selves off. I always felt that I could not understand that concept until it actually started to happen to me. It was "No, come back," you know? So it is a combined effort, and it continues to be a combined effort in every sense of the word, because I don't see where that's all that unhealthy or that I'd even want to change it, because even in work situations, stuff can get really stressful or out of control. I'm not sure if it's the Native American part of or the child part of me that can find some humor in it and some strength temporarily to pull the situation out and make a change and then go from there. So I guess there are still parts there, and OK, as long as it works in a healthy way, there you go. I believe in pulling on your inner strength and asking your ancestors to help and to push the anxiety out of your system. Some people would think this is magical thinking, but I truly believe that when you're in this state or on this level, that you can pull in other entities or other energy that will latch onto you or other spirits that haven't gone onto the light. I truly believe that, and sometimes it's as simple as that, as just sending them on to the light, so I pull on all of those things to change. Obviously, I don't do it openly and verbally, or I'd be locked up in a straitjacket. [She laughs.) *But it works, it works. I've always done that from the first time I can remember it, I was probably three when I did like a creative visualization to get out of a situation that I was in, and then I can remember using it all the time. I can also remember speaking to an elder all the time and then her telling me what to use, what to do. It's just me...See, that's why I think we can overanalyze to the point of driving ourselves insane. You know, who cares who it is? It works.*

Sarah I

Sarah I is a forty-seven-year-old, single woman with no children. She was married and divorced in her twenties. She was not diagnosed with DID until the age of thirty-five, and the therapist who made the diagnosis had not worked with DID previously. Sarah I continues to work with the same therapist.

Although she had several planned hospitalizations connected with her therapy, she maintained her employment with the same company. She has recently been promoted within the company to a team leader position. It is important to note that her employers are not aware that she has DID.

Sarah was very forthcoming and spoke at length on various topics. The session was opened with a review of the project topic.

I do need to ask a question, and I'm hoping you will expound on the question, but you know, my kids [alters] really want to be here. We've had a discussion, and I told them this is an adult thing, but they may just come and say a word or two as we talk about things…Is that OK? [She was assured this was fine.] *I'm not sure they will, but I just want to be sure that that's OK, because this morning and yesterday, I took half an hour to just reread these* [interview questions], *and several of them wanted to share with you. They may not; they're really pretty good about staying within, but they're excited about this. Well, I'm excited about this…They said that.*

I framed the project question at this point, after assuring Sarah that however she felt comfortable doing the interview was fine.

The very first thing that happened when I got this in the mail and read it was M., the teenager, wanted to know what midlife was…and that was when I explained to her what it was, that certainly midlife has impacted me…I don't feel like I'm in my midlife years. I have many younger children in me, and I feel a lot younger than in midlife. I mean, I hear forty-seven, and it doesn't compute…you know, physically, though, it does compute….And so there is that dichotomy going on and it's something I have to live with for my internal people, because they don't have midlife, but I do. The teenager, M., and the others are younger. A couple are older, but most of them are young, so that's a constant influence, and I'm, I would say, I'm maybe premenopausal, maybe. You know, I'm just barely starting to see changes, and it's something I have to work on a lot, and I'll have to work on because period cycles have forever been an issue for M., so having to go away is going to be something I think that's probably going to be received well, but also traumatizing, because it took us so long to accept it. So I do think in my external relationships that I allow the youthful feelings to be explored that I didn't have as a child. So now I'm letting myself be childlike at times, and we think more creatively and freely, all the things I associate with youth. More with youth I'm allowing myself to do that, and my external relationships are aware of that, you know, people I'm closest know who I am. All of us. I don't have to hide that. I mean, the kids don't come out, but you know, I get silly or I get giggle, and they [outside people] understand. I don't have children of my own, but my inner children are experimenting and having fun for the first time in their lives, and it's keeping midlife more fun, I think. But at the same time, I think I have to get a reality check every now and again, because I really am forty-seven, and the body really is there, so you have to do the reality check. The irony for all people like me is that your mind can stay young when your body continues to get old, and trying to accept the dichotomy is a challenge. I'm just starting life, and it's pretty wonderful. Well, I think I've lived two lifetimes. I was old-young and didn't have a life, and then I got on the healing process, and it took me a long time, but now I have a life, and I feel a lot wiser, and part of that is just my age and having lived through so many more years...I lived through enough years to get past it and on to something else, and I never believed that was possible...But not only is it possible, it happened in my life and I'm happy. The older I get, the more I love life, the better I feel about myself, the more I want to go on and on and on, because it's just really starting, and WOW, it's exciting. A huge part of why I'm here—not for this talk, but alive today—is the validation. I've lived long enough to be able to come to a very different place...And I'm strong enough to be able to share that with others who want to hear it, whatever it is, you know, just kind of the wisdom. I feel that I'm better prepared, and I really believe a lot of that is just living long enough to experience and experiment and to be willing to learn from your experiences, whether they are good or bad, they just are...They're like feelings, you know, they just are, but you can learn from them, you grow from them, and now everything to me is potential. That's how I see everything—no matter how unpleasant it might be, it's a gift, and I always learn. It used to take me years and years to see anything positive out of something "negative" that occurred, but now I'm much quicker to see that all things have positive parts.

Sarah spoke about her coworkers who are younger women and sees herself validated and accepted by their response to her, even though they do not know. She also speaks of self-acceptance, self-responsibility, and the ability to nurture.

This is a generalization, but overall, I can see a lot of things, and somehow, when I see that, it just makes me so glad to be where I am…I would trade it, but I'm much happier where I am…It's hard for me to know how much of that is my healing and how much is my age; of course, I can't separate them, it's all a part of me, but I do think my awareness is incredibly high on all things, and each time it seems that I have moved beyond, and that it's possible. People turn to me for mentoring. I feel like my expression, my ideas are educated yet sincere enough so that it might be taken for the value it's given…It feels good [referring to people who are unaware of her alters]. *Self-acceptance…and rejoicing in the different parts of me that have needs and desires, and meeting those needs, and being able to do that myself…feeling very self-sufficient or self-nurturing…I've learned to do that, and ultimately, in my mind, I feel that ultimately that's where all of us have to be fulfilled…An outside person can't be in our society. I grew up thinking if I married a man, then he would fulfill me, I would get married and live happily ever after, and somehow that magical thing, that once you were married, that life would be beautiful is what I believed in, and of course that wasn't the reality. Now I am of the belief that no one human being can fill us with the things we're missing. Only we can fill the things we're missing, and my spiritual power can do that with me.*

Not all people are born with the ability to nurture. I believe that my higher power gives us, because we are women, a different set of tools and gifts than men have. They have theirs, but it's different. And part of what makes us able to nurture is acceptance, and acceptance is about love and allowing things to be different in every child. I do believe as women we do have a connection that men have not been given. I think some of them acquire it, work hard at getting it, but it is not natural—they are not born with it.

There is a very interesting relationship that goes on between men and women in the corporate world. In my experience, men come to the table with a whole different set of ideas and thoughts...Men are more about ego and self-achieving and getting the job done, no matter what it takes. Women tend to be more about getting everyone involved and having everybody in agreement. Men tend to be more "I don't care if they agree, we'll get somebody else."...Women tend to come to that table very differently. They want everyone to be OK with it...They want that link, that connection.

I feel like we [alters] all grow together. Even though they seem to stay separate in their age, everything is done by consensus. Now that's still a chore; getting dressed in the morning can still be a challenge. H. wants to do bright red lipstick and high heels to work, and this is not OK, so we still struggle with those kinds of things, but not for very long. We come to consensus pretty rapidly now, and I really believe that's happening because all of our needs are being met.

Sarah spoke about her internal parts in terms of integration.

I don't feel as segmented as I used to, but in the process, we have all become one in the sense that we agree on things together, and we don't move forward until we're all together. And we move forward a lot, and we are ready to keep moving and growing…all of that. None of them didn't want to, and as they started to understand and cooperate and feel nurtured, the more nurtured they felt, the more I came together, just parts of me.

So now we are individualized and still think separately. I'll tell you about reading this paper [the interview guide questions] *and M.'s ideas are very distinctive, and they come through very clearly. We work together better, and we're like a team, and I feel stronger and more whole. The parts of me, it's like I'm more than one person, that's how strong I am. I'm a force to be reckoned with—in a good way. And I acknowledge that I have nurtured and developed each piece of me to a point of being healed and happy, and I don't want union* [integration of personality], *that's just how it happened for me.*

I'm a team leader at work, and I am an excellent team leader, but I didn't put it together until I read your questions, and I thought, "My God, I'm a team leader, of course I'm a team leader!" But it's ironic to me that the people who hated what was happening to me at work [the hospitalizations] and were against me, and there were people who tried to get me fired, the same people promoted me for those skills. I mean, it's pretty ironic...and I could lead them.

Sarah I needed to talk about her spiritualism, since for her it was the main element of her survival throughout the years of abuse and chaos.

Sarah is my spirit, and when she comes, she fills up my inner space. There's a warm, yellow presence in my body that fills up, and she's very wise, and she's peaceful. She was always there to help my kids [alters].

Initially, I hated them all; I wanted them all dead. So she was a big part of the nurturing; she was a big part of saying, "Give it a chance. Let this one be whatever." She's ageless. I'm not a religious person at all, but I'm a very spiritual person, and that's what connects with me...so universal...so beyond dogma. That peace fills me. I pray now. I never used to, but I pray now, and I pray because it's a feeling; it's a part of who I am, and I want people to be safe and cared for and watched out for. All of my people [alters] are spiritual. A lot of that came with the merging, the healing. I really believe that there is a spiritual dimension, and as I look back on my life, I just feel like I had angels that guided me through all of this. There were too many specific incidences where I should have been dead or something horrible, yeah, literally dead, but nothing happened... Something came in, somebody intervened, whatever it was, something occurred, and it's happened way too many times in my life for me not to believe it. We feel a lot of gratitude and a lot of accomplishment.

EVE

Eve is a thirty-eight, married with three children. She has an established career and is active in her church and town. Both Eve and her husband have graduate degrees and work within a professional community. They have high profiles in their professional and church communities. She was diagnosed with DID six years ago. Prior to that, she had no connection with the mental health profession. Eve and her husband had worked together in therapy to help him get through some personal issues of his own.

The interview began with an overview of the project and probe questions, informed consents, and releases. She had some questions about who would hear the tapes. I reassured her that myself and the transcriber (a non–mental health professional who lived several states away) would have access to the recorded interview. Eve had reviewed the material prior to

the interview and was prepared to address the topic. Most of Eve's monologue was spontaneous, needing little prompting.

*Hmmmm, I'm not entirely sure, because the whole stuff about DID kind
of came in a big wave with a lot of external factors. So, as far as change
between when I first learned and now? I was pregnant when I first knew.
I think the biggest thing that's impacted my life is just this therapy and
coping and becoming more adept at dealing with stressors and triggers.
It happens that that has come with time, so I'm kind of in the middle of,
I guess, middle age. I'm thirty-eight, and I think that I'm not sure if it's
the aging and the middle of life or the fact that this just happens to be
the time when therapy has been really fruitful and helpful and just over
time...Does that make any sense? Right now is one of the more stable
times, and I'm not sure whether to attribute it to my age and life right
now, or if it's because now is when therapy is paying off...Do you know
what I'm saying?*

*I think I'm at this point more comfortable with it now than I ever
have been. I spent a lot of time working on being comfortable with who
I am and understanding why I do the things I do...and understanding
what I can do to foster success in myself. I'm comfortable in where my
profession's at. I practice at being appreciated and regarded in my work,
and my relationship with my husband is in a pretty good state right now.*

I'm feeling secure enough to do things, to go beyond my paradigm a little in different areas that I haven't been for a while.

Eve was asked to explain what she meant about her "paradigm."

Well, there was a long period of time where we never really would do things with friends—didn't really go out, didn't really date, didn't really do anything extra. I mean, since the early periods of when I discovered I was dissociated until the last six months or a year, I started becoming a lot more comfortable with it. I don't go to therapy all the time; I take breaks when I feel like I'm OK for a while. Last year at this time, I actually considered myself done from therapy, bought myself a graduation present, and [laughs] then later went back. But I am feeling pretty comfortable with just who I am and able to make a difference in the world, able to make some change, able to use the information that I've gained to help others, not necessarily about dissociation, but in my profession, and in the volunteer stuff I do for the church. All of that is kind of just having a full life and loving life and not being buried by having DID. I don't really talk about it much, anyway…just among my other DID or MPD friends that we joke about it. But it's not like an open topic of conversation with folks, really. I think that DID gives you lots of coping strategies; you know, that's mostly a strength, mostly a good thing, and occasionally, not a good thing. You can appear to be more in tune or less in tune, depending on how connected you are. If we get really disconnected, then we're not intuitive at all...We lose all kinds of information, not picking up on subtleties that we should, kind of a scattershot. And if we are successful or not, it's kind of more by chance. Yeah, when there's a scattershot approach, if we fall back into survival kind of techniques that are maladaptive, then there's a problem.

Eve gave an example of what she meant would trigger the scattershot approach.

I'm gonna run away, or I'm gonna, you know, that kind of maladaptive stuff that's not helpful to that kind of situation. We mostly are maladaptive on the inside, so we mostly just deal. I feel like it's OK, I'm doing OK. It's very subtle. Sometimes things will happen, and we'll find out later, "Gee, that was kinda dumb." And I had no idea...It seemed fine [laughs], but then later, it's like, I don't pick up on the right away, it's like, later on I go, "Well, maybe that's not such a good thing," but...[She sighs.] Most people I work with don't know...Anybody who's a close friend knows, and some associates who I trust know, mostly through church, which is pretty safe. Not everybody's safe, but pretty safe. I don't tell people unless I know that they're going to be comfortable with it or unless I'm going to be comfortable with whatever their response is. Some people are confused by it and don't understand it, especially men. [She laughs.] *My former* [church leader], *who was there through most of it, was very, very supportive, was wonderful, and he had a gift, I think, of understanding and being a healing listener.*

The current church leader is really nice, a really wonderful guy, but I think he's—I don't know for sure—I think he's self-conscious of me, because I'm more educated than him, but he's very supportive. But then one day, he made a comment about a friend of mine who also sees my therapist, and I was just blown away...I'm like, "Where'd that come from?" and he wouldn't tell me. So I don't really trust him now. I trust him with some things, but I don't trust him with anything to do with therapy or DID, which is fine, because he's not there to be my therapist. It's not fun, but it's the way it is.

Eve talked about her spirituality at length.

I—we've—always been relatively spiritual, and we really had to rely on Father to get through the trauma early, Father in heaven. [Eve is Christian.] *We had to rely on him again in the last years, dealing with the dissociation stuff and all of the current stuff that's gone on...deaths and changes and even moving. Though we really love it here, even good change sometimes is hard. Yeah, so we rely pretty heavily on him, but it's hard, because sometimes we forget to pray. Eve's the spiritual center. I don't know that we have one leader per se, but we have a couple of people to rely on in an orchestra, because sometimes there are solos, and sometimes there are duets, and sometimes there's a whole mix of things, and sometimes they sound terrible, and sometimes they sound great, you know what I mean? Sometimes they sound good, and sometimes they sound horrible...Sure.*

If there's confusion, usually my therapist says, "What does Eve say about this?" and then Eve will go ask Father if she has questions and get an answer. She's good, yeah. I always have been spiritual, and at one point, I had stopped practicing my religion when I was nineteen or twenty...had a period of alcohol and drug abuse, and I lived with [her husband] before we were married. So about seven years ago I wanted to go back to spirituality and decided I would investigate churches and think about religion again. So then when I went back to church, then I had the feeling that I needed to live my religion in order to determine if it was right or not...I couldn't just fake it, couldn't just go but still party on the weekends or whatever. So then, I decided to live my religion, and I stopped drinking and smoking. The chemicals kept me dissociated.

Eve spoke about various life changes and how they have affected her.

All of these things—these career changes, my illness, my parents' deaths—all of that served as challenges, because each one of them brought their own issues, like, you know, my dad's death brought lots of issues up. All roads lead to Rome kind of thing, and it would just always come back to it, and it's just some other reason to deal with some other piece, just triggered all kinds of stuff. So I think in some ways, all of those things accelerated my work and make me have to rely more on spiritual strength and have to develop more spiritual strength to get through, and so those things were catalysts for more healing, even though I wouldn't wish them on anybody.

There's gotta be an easier way. I just try to turn stuff around to what's good that we got out of it. We got something good out of every-thing...but they weren't without cost.

I think we're getting older. As we have done a lot of this work, a lot of the parts have aged. Because those parts have experienced things, have experienced growth and been able to grow, so I'm feeling kind of old [laughs], kind of boring. I've worked very, very hard at it. So I think we're progressing in age. Over time, Eve has felt herself progressing in terms of internal awareness of self and internal cooperation.

Awareness, increased awareness. I think that there are many issues, but there's awareness, there's cooperation, there's love, honor, and respect...love, honor, respect is our main theme. If we get a new part or somebody gets really upset, there's help to help them deal with it, not push them down or push them back or away. What can we all learn from this? Just understanding and accepting that that's going to happen; there's a lifetime of crapola that doesn't just go nowhere, it goes somewhere, so we'll just deal with it. If you fight and don't embrace those parts, it's detrimental to me, hurtful. That part that's got this problem, if that part is just accepted unconditionally and loved and cared for: love, honor, and respect.

Five years ago, we were at the beginning stages of just learning what that meant—there was a lot of not knowing what was going on—so now I feel like I know more about what's going on to the extent that I know the process better, but it continues to evolve. So people continue to evolve, the process continues to evolve, but I feel like I have benefited from what went on five years ago. So I think five years from now, I hope and pray that I would continue to benefit from what has happened before, so that I can lead an enjoyable life and a harmonious life...and have less and less down time between difficult times that I don't anticipate will go away forever...[There was a long pause at this point.]

It was a relief when I actually found out or accepted, it was a relief because then there was an explanation for a lot of weirdness. A lot of strange things that have happened...What was that about, or how does that happen, or, you know, I wasn't crazy. [She laughs.] *So it's a good thing, and it's easier to deal with than not having it...That would be difficult. Then I would be certain I was crazy!* [She laughs.] *Integration... We call that the "I" word...We don't use it very much.* [She laughs.] *It has an awkward feeling to it, so we don't usually talk about or consider or think about it. It's kind of like I would say, "Why? What would be the point?" You know what I mean?*

Future? [Referring to terminating therapy:] *I don't...Actually, I think that it's cyclical. You know the book "Men Are from Mars, Women Are from Venus? Women are like waves. I think that is really true, and that I can get better and better, and I can get further apart from problems. As I become better, the low times are shorter, so I can come back out of it, and maybe at some point, I'll be able to do that on my own. But at this point, I see there's not a point in trying to get done with it permanently, because then I think I'm setting myself up for something that is probably not doable. Not as long, not as intense, and farther apart. Not bad...yeah, OK...probably not good by comparison to others that I don't know...I'd like to see somebody who does this really well.* [She laughs.] *Yeah, the little pieces...So, does that answer your questions? Do you have more? I think that I tried to answer this, the being in midlife with dissociative identity disorder, I don't think it's easy...*

SARAH II

Sarah II is forty, married with children. She is well educated and is a professional working in the community school system. She attends church and is involved in the community. She is currently in therapy with the therapist who diagnosed DID. Her experience with the mental health system was minimal prior to the diagnosis.

The interview opened with a review of the informed consent and signed releases. The guide questions were discussed, and Sarah was encouraged to ask for clarification at any time.

I think that when we had our fortieth birthday it got, like we didn't want to have a fortieth birthday...We thought we should have "been there" by then. We should have the career, the degree, the internal and external relationships. Somehow, it seemed like an age where when we were younger and having children, we were a young mother, and so associated with that seems to be a lot of learning, and that was OK...So we didn't know everything...Then when we were thirty, that was still OK, because we were having children that were just growing, and now our children, our outside children's ages - A is our oldest, and B is our youngest, so we kind of think, there's a lot more things that we should know…We're not as settled as we see other people our age. We don't seem to be as self-assured and to have made as much progress as other people, but yet friends and people we work with think we do just fine. It's kind of like, I don't know, it's kinda hard, because a lot of grown-up things that we should know that we don't really understand a whole lot about our- selves…and that's kind of hard…I would imagine it's real hard. Because like a lot of grown-up things we'd like to tell our [biological] *daughter, and like we should be able to tell her about things that we really don't understand. So we got some books and read them. And we talk to her a lot, because we don't want her to think that we're not interested… that it's OK that we know enough that she can feel comfortable. But something new has happened in the last year or so. A lot of it is, I think when people are forty, it seems they've got pretty much the career they want, or they at least are working toward it, and their family life is the way they want it, and they feel comfortable where they are, and that's not always true for us. A few men are changing careers, and with the economy the way it is, it's almost accepted. It feels like this is the year that we said, "OK, when we grow up, so and so will be OK." And then we realized, wait a minute…*[She laughs] *We ARE there. It's NOT OK…Now what do we do? Some people* [inside] *don't want to grow up, because it's too hard.*

Sarah's biological children do not know about her DID, and her husband thinks that she's doing "inner child" work with her therapist.

He just thinks that's something you do when you're doing your work. That it's not really a part of who we are all the time. It wasn't really hard before this year. I don't know, this year, it seems it's hardest, because we have more and more people coming out, and we also have the eldest child who only has one more year of high school. We're looking at how we've been as a mom and how we've affected him, and, you know, who he is as a person, and who he will be as he goes into the world. And although we're very proud of how he's turned out and how he is, we still stop and think about it. When people go away...we're hard with endings. Like we keep thinking we should have another child, we're not GOING to, but we're not able to get settled with that; we're not able to bring that to closure and say it's OK that we're not having any more children. When we're pregnant, we feel like we're doing something really important and really good.

Yeah, this age seems to...We just evaluate everything, always...you know? It's just like every single night we do, and sometimes it's positive, and sometimes it's really negative. We feel bad about ourselves, and we think we didn't do it right, and we're not good enough. That even though like we know we're supposed to be satisfied, we think we should be better than other people. We always had to know things that little kids

normally shouldn't have to do, so therefore we should know more...And
we figure by now, we should have it all figured out. It's harder to pre-
tend now. Like we pretend during the day when we're with other people,
and we pretend we're adult. Then we work at school as an adult, even if
we're pretending, and we're very careful to make sure that we're acting
appropriately and not acting childish, because we want to be friendly to
the children that we teach, but we don't want to be their friend, their
peer; we want to be grown-up. We don't really have, like, a real adult.
We pretend.

There's a lot of good teachers that ask for us specifically...They want
us to teach. We think that's good, but then we keep thinking, "Well, if
they really knew..." And sometimes it's hard at school, because we see a
kid, and whether or not the teacher told us, or whether we see it through
their actions, that can be really hard, because that can be triggering. And
by substituting, you're not there for a long enough period to make a real
impact, so I try to say to myself, "Well, if I can make it a really posi-
tive day," and then whenever I see that child in the hall, they generally
have a really good interaction, and they always know that I think they're
important.

Sarah was asked about other life events, like aging parents. She could not
talk about her own parents, but did mention her in-laws.

But we have my husband's parents, and they're getting older...It's getting a little bit difficult, but my husband also has a brother, and he and his wife don't have any children. So I don't know, we'll see what happens, but they don't want either family to take care of them...They want to be in a residential-type facility near one of us, so we'll see. We get along really well, but my father-in-law has always been pretty severe...and that's really hard, because it's triggering and scares us. And so I'm kinda hoping he won't ever come to live here. Now we're starting to think about that.

Sarah II is selective about who know about her DID.

We've got some parts that stutter, and we've been really careful about not stuttering in front of other people. We have a couple of friends that we're safe with. We stutter with them sometimes, and we stutter when we do our work sometimes, so we try not to come out too much. Just a few friends know. Some friends that I grew up with know that I was abused, but they don't know what kind of abuse, and they don't know how extensive, so they don't know me.

I think the world would view me as crazy...I think that at school, I think they'd feel I wasn't safe to be with the children...that they couldn't trust me. People don't understand [about DID]. Sometimes, we switch at work, and it's helpful. But we make sure there's someone that watches to make sure that if they're not OK, we can get older real quick for them...You have to anticipate where they're going and what's happening before things get there. They [employers] wouldn't trust us...They would think something was wrong with us.

We've had a few therapists off and on, but it's really hard to find one that understands us and really knows what they're doing. [She laughs.] We needed to find someone that was respectful and somebody who would honor who we are morally and spiritually...and somebody who understood about us, somebody who wasn't scared by all the chaos and horror. Because some people say, "Yeah, we work with the survivors," but when you really go to telling them stuff, they really don't want to hear it, because they can't. They didn't know. My therapist is very respectful; we've been with him four years.

And I guess what I'd really like people to know is that they need to start listening, stop saying that they have all the answers that they really don't have...I think a lot of therapists try to mask so much by medication that they never really find out either who the person is or what the problem is and want to help them really work through the problem...you know? But I think that can happen, they need to find out why they can't do it...What are they so afraid of that they won't do it? And I think a lot of that is that they'll see similarities in themselves that they don't want to have...or they shouldn't have. We do a lot of Band-Aid fixing in this society…and Band-Aids, as you know, as soon as you wash your hands, they fall off…and then what? I mean, your health insurance will give you ten or twelve visits, and that's very nice; however, I guess one of the large things I say is nobody ever minded it how many YEARS I was being abused. So why should people who have not been there be able to say, "It should only take you X amount of time, X amount of visits?" Well, nobody was saying I could only be abused that many times, you know? I find that really interesting and frustrating.

Sarah spoke about a political situation about repressed memories that took place in her state of residence. She spoke publicly before the state legislature about childhood sexual abuse and ritual abuse, even though she recognized people from "both sides." This was an empowering event for her, although it had the potential to put both her and her family at risk. Sarah talked about internal harmony and cooperation.

In ten years there'll be more harmony. And I think that, I don't know if it will be ten years from now or when it'll be, I don't know if it's gonna be a month from now. That I guess what I'm saying is that hopefully there won't be borders between people that kind of block communication sometimes.

Do we sometimes wish we didn't have parts? Yeah…Do we sometimes wish that we were "normal," whatever that may be? Yeah, we think it

*would probably be easier...I mean, we think more than other people prob-
ably do...You know, we think on overtime...Because, you know, there's
so much consensus that has to be taken a lot of times. But what do you
really tell people [inside] if you, if they have to be one, that they weren't
important enough to stay around!*

*My spiritual part is named Sarah. She's always been with me. Sarah
keeps me going and keeps things pretty much together, but she's not always
happy or always sad; she has moods, too. But Sarah is the strength that
keeps the system moving and going...like people have different jobs...
Some of them [alters] haven't...like, they don't feel like they're...well,
they felt they were so bad that they couldn't go to God and so, so some
people [alters] that can, or have, can help them to find out what they
CAN do...Yeah...*

*If you are hurtful to people inside, it only hurts them more, and it's
harder to get along, too. So let's say we have a part that's really upset
about something, and then we try to be really respectful, and we try to
allow them to be where they need to be. And if they need to cry in a corner,
and they need to be there, and they don't want anybody near them, we try
to make sure there's somebody who understands. For the most part, we
cooperate. The bottom line is that we have a safety contract with our therapist, and if we get to a point where we can't get everyone to agree upon
a safety issue, then they agree not to disagree, and they agree to adhere*

to the contract. So even if somebody told us we have to hurt ourselves because, you know, it's kind of an automatic programmed response, then it's the best that we can do is to get that person to say, "No, this is really what I have to do, but I won't do it because we do have a contract, and either I don't agree with what it says the wrong thing, blah, blah, blah, we still won't do it." Sometimes it's harder than other times [laughs], but we're getting better at it. We're realizing what it does when we don't... We realize how much hurt it causes inside...So when we really stop and look at what we don't agree about and then work it...generally, it comes through. Oh, sometimes I'm better at it than others, but that's what we're working toward.

Sarah II's final comment:

Sometimes, I think that I wish there were a day when I could stand up before a large psychiatric board and let them see who I really am, and tell them who I really am...and they'd be surprised at how many people are like me!

BETTY

Betty is forty-four, married with no children of her own. Her only previous experience with the mental health community was family counseling when she was a child. Betty spoke with little prompting and was very forthcoming in her comments on many topics. It is important to note that Betty's husband also has DID.

Yes, the biggest thing is that ten years ago we [alters] didn't realize that we were a multiple. We always knew that we were different; forever, we felt that we were different, felt that we were not like other people, but we didn't know why…And I think I was about thirty-two and a successful businesswoman, had accomplished nearly every goal that I had set for myself and got injured in an accident at work…and wasn't able to continue working…and I kind of crashed. We saw a counselor briefly, and they insisted we had to try medication, and we had problems with every medication. No more drugs, we're through it, and we were all set, but we kept having blackouts and getting mixed up about things. So they did medical tests, and they couldn't find any root and that was getting to us, again. And the doctor we were seeing for our back problems wouldn't let us work. The neurologist wouldn't let us drive because of the blackouts, but it was REALLY hard, because they didn't know why, we didn't know why. The doctor wrote his report and said we were malingerers, because on one day we had a firm handshake, and on the next day, we had a fishy handshake. The MMPI thing showed that something wasn't quite right with us, but they weren't sure just what it was.

A friend of Betty's connected her with a therapist, Jane (pseudonym), who worked with her and had Betty start keeping a journal. Betty noticed the different handwritings. So she went to the library and researched MPD and then told her therapist.

We talked to Jane, and she said that she had been aware that she felt like she was talking to different people. But she said, "I have no expertise working..."and she said "I'm willing to continue as your therapist, but you have to realize I'm limited in my knowledge, and if you decide that you want to continue on, we'll have to learn together."

Betty talked about trust, validation, and empathy issues.

You need someone that can understand and love you unconditionally through the hard times...And it's even hard for us now to actually let our child parts be out...It's easier around [husband] and around Jane, but with other people, we have to kind of keep them inside, because it's pretty weird for a forty-four-year-old woman to have a little girl's voice and to act like a two-year-old; it's weird. The people we're comfortable around let the kids come out if they want to come out...We just let ourselves be us, yeah. I did a three-month group, an all-day commitment with other multiples. OK, all of these people sitting here are just like us...They have parts, and some can work and some can't; some get along with their family, some don't; some husbands understand, some of them don't; some of them are married, some aren't. I realized, OK, all of these women have the same kind of issues, and they're all trying to do the same thing we are…They're trying to figure out how to exist and live in a world that doesn't basically understand that we're different…And even though we're different, we're still intelligent, we can still do many, many things; it's just we may have little bumps in the road.

That group really was vitally important. I made lasting friendships. And the church was concerned about survivors and invited a group of survivors to talk about survivor issues, and in that group, there ended up being five multiples. They were members of the same religion, so that was even more validating. That was empowering. When it feels right, we share we're multiple. We had friends that did go "Bleah," with everything, and people had trouble accepting it…you know, and so, it's like, you've got to be selective. It's not carte blanche; it's still kind of selective, and yet you want the message to go out. Still, in society there's that curtain, and among the people that knew, it was comfortable. My parents still do not know…No one in my family knows…Friends know, but my family does not, and someday, I'll tell them, but I had this feeling, like they're not ready to hear this…and I don't want to, and I now have a good relationship again with them.

Betty discusses internal and external acceptance.

So we want to get as many people to know about it. [A friend] *doesn't; he's now a kind of counselor at an institution. And I have to think that maybe some of the things about us have made him wonder, and it's helped him with his empathy. Now he accepts everything. He said, "Even if it's not real to me, I believe it's real to you, and I'm going to listen to what's real to you and accept that it's real to you, even though I can't understand it."*

It's all relative, isn't it? That's the part that we want the rest of the world to get to. It's that very thing…and, in a very broad sense, it doesn't happen…I mean, this tiny portion of people feel as you do, as we do, and the rest, now, like Joe [pseudonym for her husband, who has DID, too], *if they knew that he was multiple, he'd get fired…He'd lose his job; yet he is able to perform his job well…He's been there ten years… and hasn't had a problem. Yeah! You know, it's in the DSM manual as a mental illness…WE'RE NOT ILL!* [She laughs.] *Originally, we were going to become one, and now it's like, OK we have become one… one group.* [She laughs.] *I suspect through the years we will blend in and basically become one…but it's so traumatic to the child alters…They think that they're going to be murdered, even though all their parts of them, everything, is going to be put into the mix, so to speak. They can't handle it, so we say FINE…we functioned for forty-four years this way, why not forty-four more? What's the big deal? It's a nonissue…If it happens, it happens. You know, let it go how it goes. People in the world see* The Three Faces of Eve *or* Sybil, *and it looks so weird, it looks so bizarre and crazy…That's the hardest thing. A lot of people cannot accept the things that happened to us that made us be multiple. And because they can't accept those things happening, then they can't accept the fact of multiplicity. It's a remarkable adaptation how our minds, spirits, whatever, do that to protect us…Gosh, if we remembered those things when we were two, three, four years old, we would be destroyed. Multiplicity has both sides, negative and positive. But in many ways, I think it's a positive thing. The negative thing is that not everybody understands it, and because everybody doesn't understand it, you can't bring into the open. We have great acceptance on the inside…That was very hard to achieve, but now I really feel like there's a great deal of acceptance…Sometimes we have to be reminded.*

Betty talks about becoming "real," her Pinocchio concept.

In some ways I think it's just understanding ourselves better through years of therapy and experience…But, I don't know, it's a lot different right now. Here I am, I'm beginning to feel less emotionally handicapped, but the physical handicaps [old physical injuries from accidents] *are still there, but the people that are used to anesthetization, they say go ahead, go back to work, we'll take care of it...I think, "No, I don't want to do that. This is our body, even though we don't feel that we hurt it, it's still feeling it even though we don't feel it..." It's hard to get real, because it's automatic to protect. Say this arm hurts, so, we'll numb it up, you go right ahead. So it's hard to turn off the switch and to become the person in control of their own life. We call it Pinocchio syndrome...to be a real boy...It's after forty years of being on automatic.*

We're definitely changing, and we know we're changing, and we're starting to become a real boy, you know, our Pinocchio thing, our image, we're starting to become a real person, and it's OK now...It's OK if everybody feels sad or everybody feels happy. In my little circle [external and internal relationships], *I feel very safe. We want things to be real now.*

Betty shared her spirituality concept and its impact on her life.

We've always had strong religious beliefs. Ever since we were like five or six years old...We all feel good about it, we feel comfortable within, and we like it. I think that that spiritual base was important and is important to us as a system. It's a group thing, but [alter], *she's kind of the most spiritual one, kind of in charge. We'd be different people, very different people, we believe that the things that happened to us were wrong…And we believe that God will take care of that in his own way, in his own time, that we're not responsible to them, and, although it's fine for us to be angry with what happened, it's not right for us to judge their actions, because we don't know why they took those actions. So, we can accept what happened to us was wrong, and that it will be taken care of…I think, without the spiritual side, we might have been tempted to act out inappropriately and do harmful things in return…But we had this peace that they will get their proper judgment or whatever. We feel it's important to help, to help other people that have suffered the same kinds of things…It feels to us that if we don't have good come of it, then it's been a total waste. That's it, we're excited for this opportunity to participate because hopefully, this information may in some way reach someone else, and some good can come of it. It feels like, if we just took everything that happened and just kept it in a little box, then we're in error, because no one else in any way gets any benefit of what happened, of our experience…Because of our experience of sharing, a mother realized her daughter had been molested.*

Betty talked about her marriage and how life changed for her.

OK, so we got married…Well, when we got married, this was a whole new level of security, more trust issues, and yet it felt like I was complete now. I have a partner, and my whole life changed...I didn't have the same financial worries, because I had a regular income again now. We, I got married at forty—life begins at forty! How could it get any better than this! But this was a whole new chapter, because now I was a wife, a stepmother, and we had our own home. Had my own car. Yeah...and this was great...and, because of the security that we felt in the relationship, we were able to do more of our work...and we always wanted to be married. We always wanted to be a mother.

An addendum to this interview occurred on the way out, after the recording machine was shut down. Both Betty and her husband talked about humor and how much humor plays in their individual functioning and in their relationship. For both of them, humor has always been an important aspect of their lives.

This concludes the interviews of the six women. Each transcript is verbatim, with only names and places being changed where necessary.

CHAPTER 4

Summary

● ● ●

THE TOPIC OF THE PROJECT was conceived from my clinical experience working with midlife women with DID who kept stating frustration with life as they were experiencing it in their middle age. They expressed that "nobody gets it," referring mainly to the professional community: "I'm losing it." "It wasn't like this before." The data suggest that the internal frustration is generated by misdiagnosis and their increasing awareness of their internal organization.

Midlife was acknowledged as a pathway of life during which the women had all reached a point of acceptance and general satisfaction with their lives. Acceptance meant acceptance of their experience of living life with DID in a society that does not understand. Acceptance did not mean a trouble-free existence but was an acknowledgment of self, the difficulties of DID, and the use of learned appropriate coping skills versus maladaptive skills to manage the symptoms of DID during critical times. The journey to acceptance was long and arduous and continues to be a challenge.

The participants share four specific criteria: gender, DID, midlife, and fiscal independence. They are all survivors of severe, long-term childhood physical and sexual abuse. Their individual childhood traumas varied, but the end result was the same. They have all maintained fiscal independence, some more easily than others, during the critical times, but all six women are fiscally solvent in their current lifestyles now. Fiscal independence was defined as not being financially dependent on social services networks at the state and/or federal levels. Their fiscal independence was the criterion by which they were considered to be well functioning for this study. The study did not include marginalized groups, cross-cultural groups, or men.

The conclusion/summation of the data was less about the impact of midlife on the lives of the women and more representative of the importance of *connections* and *relationships* in their lives—externally and internally.

Jaybee talks about internal and external acceptance as being important: "Because we've been accepted—We've accepted ourselves...I have some other friends that have accepted me and all of us [her internal system]...and accepted me out here, too, So I think that acceptance alone has calmed us down."

Mato, who has been in the health profession working closely with peers for more than twenty years, states, "I can work and be focused and function and feel good about that and then have a day off. So it's hard to keep that balance and remind myself. But don't we all struggle with something emotional or whatever?" She also is selective about sharing her DID: "Obviously, I don't do it openly and verbally, or I'd be locked up in a straitjacket. But it works."

Sarah I talks about loving life: "A huge part of why I'm here—not for this talk, but alive today—is validation. I've lived long enough to be able to come to a very different place…And I'm strong enough to be able to share that with others who want to hear it, whatever it is, you know, just kind of the wisdom." She further states, "People turn to me for mentoring. I feel like my expression, my ideas are educated yet sincere enough so that it might be taken for the value it's given…It feels good [referring to people who are unaware of her alters].

Eve talked about work and her church volunteer work. "All of that is kind of just having a full life and loving life and not being buried by having DID. I don't really talk about it much, anyway…just among my other DID or MPD friends that we joke about it. But it's not like an open topic of conversation with folks, really." Sarah II also mentions work, in that she interacts and connects with coworkers and students, but is careful about revealing DID: "There's a lot of good teachers that ask for us specifically… They want us to teach. People don't understand (about DID)…Sometimes, we switch at work, and it's helpful."

In retrospect, connections and relationships were always important, but the women were not cognizant of the importance of relationships until they were correctly diagnosed in their middle years. It was at this point that they were able to begin the process of reconnection with self and others and acknowledge the traumatic disruption of past relationships/connections that had threatened their sanity and skewed their ability to formulate growth-fostering relational images during childhood, adolescence, and young adulthood (Bowlby, 1988; Jordan et al., 1991; Liotti, 1995; Miller & Stiver, 1997).

After correct diagnosis, validation, acceptance, respect, and non-judgmental regard within relationships were the primary issues that impacted the internal and external relationships, not the event of midlife. Appropriate nurturing relationships were the essential elements that gave these women a sense of connection to self and others.

The life events of children leaving home, aging and/or dying parents, personal health issues, and perimenopause/menopause during the middle passage had made internal and external adjustments in relationships necessary. The data did not support the premise that the midlife path was an exceptional event in their lives. For five of the six women, life in the here and now of middle age is a positive experience, with the inconvenience of menopause factored into the equation of living. Midlife seemed to be basically a nonissue. Most of the women are looking forward to growing and aging, now that they have some meaningful relationships and understand themselves better.

Another primary theme expressed was a strong spirituality that has been with them from the beginning of their dissociative processes. Their internal relationships with the spiritual parts of themselves was one of the primary factors that kept them alive and sane during the abusive times. Two used the names of their spiritual parts as their pseudonyms. This indicated to me how important these connections had been and continue to be for them.

Freud stated that little girls and adult women suffer from penis envy throughout their lives and live life in dependency and service to men. Without dissecting and qualifying "connection" or "relationships," Freud is correct in a broad sense; females and males live in relationship connections with others throughout their lives and are interdependent. This is a means of surviving and thriving for males and females within their cultural and societal circles. The references made to quality and types of relationships within home, work, volunteer situations, and therapy suggest an ongoing interdependence is necessary. Although they rarely chose to share the fact of having a dissociative disorder, they still have interacted with others within social situations. This does not suggest that they have always been successful socially, but that this is a work in progress.

Jaybee comments, "I have some other friends that have accepted me and all of us [internal system]. and accepted me out here, too. So I think that acceptance alone has calmed us down." Later she comments, "I was seeing a little bit of change within all of us, because we were relating." Her final comment: "I think in my case, anyway, it's getting better; it's getting better for the people on the outside of me and getting better for the people inside of me."

Sarah I talks about external relationships: "I allow the youthful feelings to be explored that I didn't have as a child...People I'm closest know who I am. All of us. I don't have to hide that." Then she comments about her position at work: "My God, I'm a team leader, of course I'm a team leader and there were people who tried to get me fired, the same people promoted me for those skills. I mean, it's pretty ironic...and I could lead them."

Eve talks about being comfortable with herself. "I spent a lot of time working on being comfortable with who I am and understanding why I do the things I do...and understanding what I can do to foster success in myself. I'm comfortable in where my profession's at. I practice at being appreciated and regarded in my work, and my relationship with my husband is in a pretty good state right now."

Sarah II mentions, "We have a couple of friends that we're safe with... Just a few friends know." Sarah II purposely uses her younger alters at work to relate to her students; she is aware that if her employers knew, her employment status would be at risk.

Betty clearly states, "When it feels right, we share we're multiple... You've got to be selective...and yet you want the message to go out. Still, in society there's that curtain, and among the people that knew, it was comfortable." Betty's husband, who also had DID, is selective about sharing the diagnosis, too. "If they (his employers) knew...he'd get fired...he'd lose his job; yet he is able to perform his job well...been there ten years... and hasn't had a problem."

The women talked about how vitally important it had been for them to be in relationships with therapists who respectfully acknowledged their experiences of life as women having DID. Several therapists admitted to having limited knowledge or treatment experience with DID but were willing to learn. This exemplifies mutual empowerment, which is developed through reciprocal attentiveness and responsiveness (Jordan et al., 1991; Miller & Stiver, 1997).

The therapist who embraces the relational model fosters a mutual sense of understanding, inquisitiveness, and unconditional respect and regard with the therapeutic relationship. "We are emphasizing the importance of a two-way interactional model, where it becomes as important to understand as to be understood, to empower as well as to be empowered"

(Surrey, 1991, p. 59). This leads to increased self-esteem for client and therapist.

Corrective changes begin to occur as the building of the therapeutic relationship progresses externally. It is a parallel process. The relationships were not like this before; this was foreign. The "interactive validation" between therapist and client becomes the template for internal awareness, cooperation, and respect. Surrey (1991) further states that "the capacity to learn to 'see' the other and to 'make oneself known' to the other highlights one's own self-knowledge and fosters growth in the other and in the self" (p. 58). For the women, this was an evolutionary process, internally and externally, and was not a smooth procedure, as the therapists would often be challenged by their DID clients.

This new way of being in relationship explained the frustrations expressed in statements such as "I'm losing it; nobody gets it; it wasn't like this before." The passage of time, self-knowledge and self-acceptance brought the awareness of the lack of acceptance and knowledge with the professional (i.e., medical, legal, religious, psychological) and social communities. The lack of connection with the outside world become more apparent, but a therapeutic connect that provided a secure base began the transformation that led to reconnecting with self and others in a cooperative and conscious manner. This was not about integration as defined by the mental health professional or in the professional literature. The women were referring to a conscious connection, respect, and cooperation within themselves as it happened within their therapy and then generalized to other relationships. They chose to retain their internal systems, adjusting the internal relationships to maintain adaptive functioning in their lives.

Conclusion

● ● ●

THIS PROJECT WAS SMALL AND limited, focusing on well-functioning women. It did not address cross-cultural or gender differences or the political implications of the misuse of power.

The value of the project is in its application of a relational approach to a specific psychological phenomenon whose pathology is created from broken, disempowering, and power-over relationships (Miller, 1976). The fact that integration of alter parts had a low priority for the women may indicate a need for clinicians to consider alternative treatment goals for DID. Another value is that the data was not manipulated to fit a specific category. Their individual words/voices were heard and reported verbatim. They spoke for themselves.

A nonjudgmental awareness and openness to the experience of being invited into the world of DID with mutual empathy and empowerment replacing the traditional neutral stance of therapy will encourage the formation of healthy relationships. Boundaries within the therapeutic frame always need to be clear and maintained in all therapeutic relationships, noting that it is not an equal relationship, no matter what the issues brought to the room may be.

The motivating factor for the women was the opportunity to be heard, which fulfilled their sense of social responsibility in a credible manner. Their enthusiasm for participating suggests a lack of credible forums within which to educate professionals and the general public. The public awareness and education about the impact of childhood sexual abuse is still understated. The examples given of how they live their lives in spite of their past traumas lend hope to all survivors, known and unknown.

REFERENCES

Belenky, M.F., Clinchy, B.M., Goldberger, N.R., & Tarule, J.M. (1986). Women's ways of knowing: The Development of self, voice and mind. New York: Basic Books.

Borysenko, J. (1996). *A woman's book of life: The biology, psychology, and spirituality of the feminine life cycle.* New York: Riverhead Books.

Bowlby, J. (1988). *A secure base: Parent-child attachment and healthy human development.* New York: Basic Books.

Briere, J. (1997). *Psychological assessment of adult posttraumatic states.* Washington, DC: American Psychological Association.

Chase, T. (1987). *When rabbit howls.* New York: Jove Books.

Chu, J. A., & Dill, D. L. (1990). Dissociative symptoms in relation to childhood physical and sexual abuse. *American Journal of Psychiatry,* 147, 887–892.

Crabtree, A. (1985). <u>Multiple man: Explorations in possession & multiple personality</u>. Ontario, Canada: Collins Publishers.

Crabtree, A. (1992). Dissociation and memory: A two-hundred year perspective, <u>Dissociation</u>, 5(3), 150-154.

Gainer, K. (1994). Dissociation and schizophrenia: An historical review of conceptual development, and relevant treatment approaches. <u>Dissociation</u>, 7(4),261-271.

Gilligan, C. (1992). *In a different voice: Psychological theory and women's development*. Cambridge, MA: Harvard University Press.

Greer, G. (1992). *The change: Women, aging and the menopause.* New York: Alfred A. Knopf.

Greer, G. (1999). *The whole woman.* New York: Alfred A. Knopf.

Hall, C. S. (1979). *A primer of Freudian psychology.* New York: New American Library.

Hillman, J. (1996<u>). *The soul's code: In search of character and calling.* </u> New York: Random House.

International Society for the Study of Dissociation. (1994). *Guidelines for treating dissociative identity disorder (multiple personality disorder) in adults.* Skokie, IL: Author.

Jordan, J. V. (1991). The meaning of mutuality. In J. V. Jordan, A. G. Kaplan, J. B. Miller, I. P. Stiver, & J. L. Surrey (Eds.), *Women's growth in connecting: Writings from the Stone Center* (pp.81–96). New York: Guilford Press.

Jordan, J. V., Kaplan, A. G., Miller, J. B., Stiver, I. P., & Surrey, J. L. (1991). *Women's growth in connection: Writings from the Stone Center.* New York: Guilford Press.

Keyes, D. (1981). The minds of Billy Milligan. New York: Random House.

Kluft, R. (1984a). An introduction to multiple personality disorder. Psychiatric Annals, 14(1), 19-24.

Kluft, R. (1984b). Aspects of the treatment of MPD. Psychiatric Annals, 14(1), 51-55.

Kluft, R., & Fine, C. (Eds.). (1993). Clinical perspectives on multiple personality disorder. Washington, DC: American Psychiatric Press.

Levinson, D. J. (1996). *The seasons of a woman's life*. New York: Ballantine Books.

Liota, G. (1995). Disorganized/disoriented attachment in the psychotherapy of the dissociative disorders. In S. Goldberg, R. Muir, & J. Kerr (Eds.)., Attachment theory: Social, developmental, and clinical perspectives (p. 343-363. Hillsdale, NJ: The Analytic Press.

Miller, J. B. (1976). *Toward a new psychology of women*. Boston: Beacon Press.

Miller, J. B. & Stiver, I. P. (1997) *The healing connection: How women form relationships in therapy and in life*. Boston: Boston Press.

O'Brien, P. (1985). The diagnosis of multiple personality syndromes: Overt, covert, and latent. Comprehensive Therapy, 11(7), 59-66.

Putnam, F. W. (1989a). *Diagnosis and treatment of multiple personality disorder*. New York: Guilford Press.

Putnam, F.W. (1989b). Pierre Janet and modern views of dissociation. Journal of Traumatic Stress, 2, 413-429. (From PTSD Research Quarterly, 1997, Summer, Abstract No. 13.)

Putnam, F.W., Guroff, J.J., Silberman, E.K., Barban, L. & Post, R.M. (1986). The clinical phenomenology of multiple personality disorder: Review of 100 recent cases. Journal of Clinical Psychiatry, 47, 285-293.

Rivera, M. (1996). More alike than different: Treating severely dissociative trauma survivors. Toronto, Canada: University of Toronto Press.

Ross, C.A. (1994). The Osiris complex: Case studies in multiple personality disorder. Toronto, Canada: University of Toronto Press.

Ross, C.A, Anderson, G., Fleisher, W.P., & Norton, G.R. (1991). The frequency of multiple personality disorder among psychiatric inpatients. American Journal of Psychiatry, 148(12, 1717-1720.

Ross, C.A.., Anderson, G., Fraser, G.A., Reagor, P., Bjornson, L., & Miller, S.D. (1992) Differentiating multiple personality disorder and dissociative disorder not otherwise specified. Dissociation 5, 88-91.

Ross, C.A., Norton, G.R. & Fraser, G.A. (1989). Evidence against the iatrogenesis of multiple personality disorder. Dissociation, 2, 61-65.

Ross, C. A. (1997). *Dissociative identity disorder: Diagnosis, clinical features and treatment of multiple personality.* New York: John Wiley & Sons.

Schreiber, F. (1973). *Sybil.* New York: Regenery.

Sheehy, G. (1995). *New passages: Mapping your life across time.* New York: Random House.

Sizemore, C. C. (1989). *A mind of my own: The woman who was known as Eve tells the story of her triumph over multiple personality disorder.* New York: Random House.

Steinem, G. (1992). *Revolution from within: A book of self-esteem.* Boston: Little, Brown and Company.

Surrey, J. L. (1991). The self-in-relation: A theory of women's development. In J. V. Jordan, A. G. Kaplan, J. B. Miller, I. P. Stiver, & J.L. Surrey (Eds.), *Women's growth in connection: Writings from the Stone Center* (pp. 51–66). New York: Guilford Press.

Thigpen, C., & Cleckley, H. M. (1957). *The three faces of Eve.* New York: McGraw-Hill.

Valillant, G. E. (1989). Images in Psychiatry: John Bowlby, 1907–1990. *American Journal of Psychiatry*, 153(11), 1483.

Wilbur, C. (1985). The effect of child abuse on the psyche. In R. P. Kluft (Ed.), *Childhood antecedents of multiple personality* (pp. 21–25). Washington, DC: American Psychiatric Press.

Van der Hart, O. (1996). Ian Hacking on Pierre Janet: A critique with further observations. Dissociation, 9(1), 80-84.

Van der Kolk, B.A. (1987). Psychological trauma. Washington DC: American Psychiatric Press.

Vander Kolk, B.A., & van der Hart, O. (1991). The intrusive past: The flexibility of memory and the engraving of trauma. American Imago, 18(4), 425-454.

Author Biography

● ● ●

Elizabeth M. W.-B. Green, PhD

LCMHC, MA, NCC, DCC, MFLC

I HAVE BEEN IN THE helping professions for approximately thirty years, starting as an emergency medical technician for ten years and then as a licensed mental health professional. I have worked many years in a private residential school working with adolescents and adults while also in private practice working with adults.

I live in rural New Hampshire with my husband of many years and two large dogs. Although basically retired, I meet with several clients in private practice. I believe strongly that mental health care should be affordable and the parameters of care not dictated by a third-party payer.

Many years ago, my doctoral dissertation was conceived by the work I had been doing with (mostly) women survivors of incredible physical and sexual abuse throughout their childhood into young adulthood.

They are amazing individuals, and I have always felt honored to be entrusted with their journeys into lives well lived. They are all unique individuals who taught me how they survived and basically needed some-one to listen to their stories without pressure, judgment, or fixing. The building of a trusting therapeutic frame took as long as two years before they could make the leap into trusting me with their internal worlds.